THROUGH *Sheila's* EYES

*As I see it, from the poems and
paintings of Sheila Simpson*

IAN McD SIMPSON

Tellwell Talent
www.tellwell.ca

ISBN
978-0-2288-3768-8 (Hardcover)
978-0-2288-3767-1 (Paperback)

What would the world be, once bereft
Of wet and wildness? Let them be left,
O let them be left, wildness and wet,
Long live the weeds and the wilderness yet.
– Gerard Manley Hopkins

PROLOGUE

Sheila was always writing during our almost fifty-eight years of married life spent happily together — and also earlier in life. She died in September 2018 at age eighty-five from Alzheimer's disease. Tidying up and finding and disposing of items has been time-consuming and at times difficult, but often it has been a great and unexpected pleasure.

Barbara Ann, Sheila's caregiver and best friend during the last few years, has been a great help. We have a very big collection of books, and Barbara Ann has discovered that many have letters and writings tucked away between the pages. We have no idea when she wrote each poem, but sometimes we can see why. Often there seems to be a connection between the book and the item inserted. Sometimes the letter, recipe, or poem inserted goes back twenty to thirty years, so this habit was not part of her illness. I have even found an envelope with the title "Poems written by Sheila Little age 11. – not very good." Some of these have a child's reflection on World War II, still raging at the time she wrote these, and of country life at that time.

At the back of our garage, my son Angus found a folder with several of Sheila's writings; it was the first of these that formed my determination to collect her poems and prose and put them together in a book. I wish I could collect all her paintings as well. Some will be a part of this book.

The first writing that I found is the one that spoke to me and asked me to preserve it. Sheila labelled it: "The Earth is a home for all people."

The next find was in one of her sketchbooks. I idly skimmed through the pages of drawings and watercolours and then turned the book over and found that all the reverse pages told the story of Brynn, our dog, and the drama of her first year.

I remember the strange way that Brynn arrived in our family.

Sheila was collecting for the Kidney Foundation and calling on the homes around our village. She visited this new resident, and when the door was opened by the lady of the house, Sheila saw newspaper around the door mat.

"Are you house-training a puppy?" she asked, recognizing the signs. At that point two puppies came tumbling out from a back room. "Oh, they are gorgeous. You'll easily find homes for them."

"I think I have a home for the ginger one, but not for the one with dark fur. And we will probably have to go back to Ontario for work. My husband is a roofer and he's not getting much work here in Corner Brook," said this new resident in Humber Village.

"Well, if you can't find a home for them, you let me know. We've got a very old dog and we will soon need another," commented Sheila.

Dougall, our dog, was sixteen or seventeen years old. He had been brought home by my son Mark, who had found him loose in Terra Nova National Park where Mark worked as a park warden. At that time, our local vet thought that he was between eighteen months and two years old. By now, fifteen or sixteen years later, he was getting stiff and old. He needed help occasionally to get back up on his hind legs.

Sheila got a phone call a week later and learned that neither puppy had a home, and the owners were soon going back to Ontario. As soon as I got home from work, Sheila urged me back into the car and off to see the dogs.

"I will let the dog decide which one I will have, and I think Rebecca [our daughter] will take the other if it has no home," Sheila said.

I knew she fancied the golden one, but as soon as I drove in, the puppies came tumbling out and the dark one immediately jumped into the car before we got out.

"Well, there you have it!" I said. "This dog has decided."

"No!" Sheila said. "We will get out of the car and play for a bit to get to know them first." But I knew she wanted the golden one, and that is the one we got, and Sheila called her Brynn. Rebecca took the dark one and called her Willow!

I had forgotten many of the stories of Brynn's first years. She was a challenging puppy to train. But I remember that in Sheila's last few years, Brynn hardly ever left her side. She sat so close that we would hear Sheila saying, "Brynn, get off my feet. I can't move." Brynn would actually find one of Sheila's feet to sit on. From being a very difficult young dog, she had become the perfect friend and companion for Sheila's last years. Barbara Ann still comments to me about the closeness of their bond.

Willow, her sister, is still alive and fit, and she spends a lot of the day with me until Rebecca picks her up to go home.

From the moment we brought Brynn home, there was a change in Dougall. It was as if (in our imagination!) he had said to himself, "OK. I will have to teach this young pup the rules and regulations here." He got back on his legs without needing assistance. He was a great help and example, and, when required, a disciplinarian. As I read Sheila's sketchbook-journal, I realized what an interesting year we had spent with Brynn.

Photo of Dougall, age seventeen, and Brynn, age one.

Dougall died two years later, and we think he was nearly twenty years old. Brynn died just a year after Sheila died. They were two great friends.

Much later I found this poem, written in red ink, in bold handwriting. Sheila had used a sheet of my office notepaper.

Between Bats and Rats our house shares Light with trees;
With Chickens and Dogs, we share our freedom.
With Moose and Birds, we share the hope of the orchard.
The trees shed their leaves.
We grow our food with help from our chickens.
The bees share our blackberry vines,
And ensure rich glowing berries to eat with our own honey.
The wind dries our clothes, and at the same time
Shakes the yellow tomato flower and sets the fruit.
And all the time the worms in the dark moist earth tunnel and munch,
And the earth becomes loose and fertile.
And the stream and ponds lush with growth
Reflect the Light that fills our lives.

I had not read this poem previously. But from the comments about chickens and bees, and the mention of stream and ponds, I think this poem was written in the late 1980s. We moved to Humber Village in 1979, at a time when Sheila seemed quite ill. We and her physician had decided that the smoke from the pulp and paper mill (and all the chemicals it contained) was contributing to her increasing illness. The move was the best thing we could have done, although it took me a few years to adjust to my twenty-minute commute! I had been spoiled by living so close to the office and hospital.

The bats arrived and spent the summers behind the twelve-inch fascia boards in the eaves. It was very interesting seeing them stream out in their dozens at dusk, and then come back at dawn. But then, during their second summer in their new home, the occasional bat used to get in the house, and one announced his presence by flopping onto Sheila's ironing board as she was ironing. The time had come to try to remove the colony.

We waited until autumn when the colony usually disappeared into hibernation. I had fine mesh placed to block the space between the fascia board and the wall. It worked. Next spring, in a home farther away and alongside the river, the owner announced they had suddenly gotten a plague of bats and needed an exterminator. We tried to persuade him to find a way to block the entrances and impressed on him that bats are a wonderful species and under threat in many places. Sadly, I think the exterminator was enlisted, but this was understandable, as bats are not very pleasant to have fluttering around inside the house at night!

Shortly after the bats, we noticed that we had rats burrowing under our chicken pen. We used to go to the chicken coop after dark, and as soon as we switched a light on, rats were scurrying away and out. We used to take our two dogs, Hobo and Tinker, and most nights they would catch one or two rats, but it wasn't enough to get rid of them. So eventually I had to use warfarin. I put some in a long three-inch pipe, half-buried near and under the compost heap. Once the rats were gone, they never came back.

We found these two dogs who were almost run over by me as I drove with Mark into Corner Brook one Saturday morning. They were very young. As they were wrestling on the edge of the road, they had rolled, entangled, onto the road. I stopped and we picked them up, turned round, and went home. We had not intended to keep them, as we had an elderly Newfoundland dog, but when we phoned the SPCA dog pound we found that it was closed for the long holiday weekend. By the Tuesday we had decided that if we could not find the owners, we would keep them. I took them to Dr. Klevorik, the local veterinarian. His receptionist told us that a lady had told her that she had seen a white van stop at the point where we picked up the dogs. The two dogs were tossed out of the van, and the van drove on.

We called them Hobo and Tinker as they seemed like hitchhikers needing help.

The following is a true and sad limerick to a brave
dog from Sheila Simpson, Humber Village:

HOBO

An old dog in Humber Village
Lost her bark due to plunder and pillage.
She was steadfast and brave
And determined to save
Her neighbour's garbage from spillage.

She barked from midnight to morning.
But her neighbour slept through the warning.
While out in his truck
A BLACK BEAR ran amuck
Shredding chip bags and wrappers till dawning.

But Hobo kept on, though she'd pay
In a very unfortunate way,
For her vocals diminished
Until they were finished;
And she's not barked again to this day.

Angus, our oldest son, had a summer job working on a hiking trail at Blomidon Brook at the base of the Blomidon Mountains. He came home after work one day with two young ducks given to him by a lady in Frenchman's Cove, a community near Angus's trail. Her flock had increased, and she had some youngsters to get rid of. The male we named Sir Francis Drake, and the female was called Jemima (Puddle-Duck).

There is a poem in Sheila's handwriting on the blank back page of *100 British Poets*, edited by Selden Rodman:

> It's very odd at half past four,
> To have ducks knocking at your door.
> In fact, it clearly seemed to be
> That they had come to call for tea,
> For we'd just put the kettle on,
> And we could hear its bubbling song.
> The dogs were full of doggy food;
> The cat was sleeping in the sun.
> So, if Sir Francis Drake and bride
> Decided they should come inside
> Perhaps we should have given them tea
> All cozy with the family.

"With Moose and Birds we share the hope of the orchard," Sheila wrote.

During the early days of living in Humber Village there were always moose to be seen. In our early years here a mother moose always delivered her calves in the village, in one of the forested areas not yet built on. And for several years she had twins.

This photo was taken in our back yard, and it is Sheila's washing line on which they are scratching.

This photo is in early spring, and the last patch of snow is visible. This was probably in the early 1980s. The mother moose has not yet pushed her twin yearlings away; she will do so when she is about to calve again.

Sheila's painting of the same washing line in late summer –
many years after the moose had left the village.

SHEILA'S POEMS

FOUND JANUARY 2020 IN A SMALL FOLDER while sorting out her papers with an explanation, in her writing (or perhaps her mother's): "Poems written by Sheila Little age 11. – not very good."

C IS FOR CHARLIE

Charlie was an aeroplane
Who lived at squadron C,
And every time when he went out
He used to take his tea,

Petrol was his bread
And oil was his cake.
With his chugging engines
He a cup of tea did make.

He'd shoot down German bombers
While eating up his bread,
And when he ate his cake
He'd shoot a fighter down instead.

When he drunk his tea
With a loud chug in his throttle

He sent another to the sea,
And finished up the bottle.

SIR BRIAN

Sir Brian was a Knight
A Chivalrous knight of old
The story I'm about to tell
Will make your blood run cold.

One day when he was riding
He heard a maiden cry,
"Help help, for I am now beset
Oh is there no help nigh?"

He looked up and beheld her
A beauteous maiden there
Her eyes were deepest blue
And golden was her hair.

She lay there on the ground
Her hands and legs were tied
But not a sound she made
The knight thought she had died.

He gently cut the bonds
And with water from a pool
He sprinkled her sweet face
With a drop of it so cool

At last she did revive
With a smile upon her lips.
He thanked God she was still alive
And gave her a few more sips.

The next day they were wed

In a church not far away
And lived happily ever after
Until their dying day.

THE GUINEA PIG WHO HAD NOT GOT A TAIL

There was a little guinea pig
Who had not got a tail.
So every day when it got dark
He used to sit and wail.

A fairy chanced to hear him as she was passing by;
Took pity on the poor young pig, and said she'd have a try
To make a curly tail for him
So he never more need cry.

All day she spent a-mixing,
And chanting magic spells
To see if she could really make
A proper tail with curls.

And after stewing toads' eyes
And making horrid smells
She really truly did succeed
In making a tail with curls.

The little pig was so amazed
When he saw the curly tail,
That splash!! He fell right into
A dirty water pail.

The fairy helped him out again
And put the new tail on
And now he squeals and plays all day
And his dismal nights are gone.

THE GYMKHANA

To the Gymkhana let us all go.
And watch the horses trot to and fro.
There will be jumping and racing too
Perhaps some bending. — That's hard to do.

The riders there will shout Gee-up or Whoa
When the horses won't stand or won't go
I'm told that some cowboys are going there too,
And one of them is taking his lasso.

Some of the horses that go there get frightened,
So the reins by the riders have to be tightened,
Or else they start bucking and prancing about
Then the judges will say "Take that horse out!"

So to the gymkhana let all of us go
To watch all the horses trot to and fro
I'm sure we'll enjoy it and like it so much
That the horses will all want us to Pat and Touch

THE HUNT

The old Inn stood on the village green,
A picturesque and pleasant scene,
With its whitewashed walls and old oak door,
And its quaint old roof all thatched with straw.

A clatter of hoofs is heard, and then
Down the road came horses and men.
Coats of red, and hats of black.
The hounds all barking, a merry pack.

Then to the Inn they made their way
To drink a toast to a merry day

In a flagon of good brown sparkling ale
While the horses drink water from the pail.

Then into the saddle they spring again,
And went down the road in a long, coloured train.
They skirted the wood and away they went
Until all the hounds had picked up the scent.

Over the hill, and over the plain.
Then the fox turned and came back again.
Into the water he plunged and crossed
So the hounds for a moment the scent had lost.

They leaped the stream and found the scent,
And the horses behind jumped, and over they went
Except for one grey who slipped as he jumped
And into the water his master he dumped.

The hounds ahead pulled fox down near his earth
And he barked and howled for all he was worth
The hounds around him were yelping and baying,
And leaping and jumping and barking and playing.

The riders came up and without more ado
They cut off his mask and his bushy tail too.
They presented them to the man who they thought
Had best ridden that day in the gay hunting sport.
Then back to the inn they went at last
Well revenged on Reynard's wicked past.

VE Day

Now that victory day is here
Flags are out, and people cheer.
Everywhere the bells are ringing.
And the nation's hearts are singing.

"God save the King" the people cry.
Let all the foes before him die,
And in the church loud voices raise
To sing to God a song of praise.

Little children in the street
Let off fireworks. What a treat!
While older boys a bonfire make
And put old Hitler there to bake.

And later in the evening when
The lamps are lit, the girls and men
All dancing on the village green
Make a bright and merry scene.

And now it's dark the stars all shine
They all go home and have some wine
And drink a toast to lasting peace
While thanking God that wars will cease.

I think this poem that follows (which I have just found) may have been written while Sheila was still at school, or perhaps after she had started teaching in England. The ink is beginning to fade, and the writing is more looped and cursive than her later writing.

EXAMINATIONS

What is it that comes round each year,
In the summer months so fair,
Wrecking the peace of the sunny hours
With work beyond compare?

What is it that causes that worried frown,
On the fairest schoolgirl's brow?
Endless night, full of question marks
Where did it happen, and how?

What is it that instigates fond Mammas,
To advise a generous dose
Of some evil-smelling tonic wine
To restore the bloom to her rose?

What is it that causes that endless hush,
Which persists throughout the school
Of mistresses padding on silent feet
All looking so calm and cool?

What is it that causes the wretched girls
To quiver and quake at the knees,
While hot and cold shivers run down their backs
And all knowledge departs with the breeze?

What is it that causes those groans and sighs,
Hot tears and wild protestations?
Why, the bane of every schoolgirl's life
Oh, those dreadful examinations.

This painting is of Toddington Parish church. I do not remember on
which year or on which holiday Sheila painted this. She and I were married
there on November 5th 1960. Her two sisters were married in this church.
Angus, our eldest child, was christened there in 1961. The funeral services
for my father, Sheila's parents, and Barbara — Sheila's younger sister —
took place in this church. This view is from the rear of the church.

Poplars Nursery, Sheila's birthplace and home.

This must have been one of Sheila's early paintings. The heap of coal tells us that this may have been painted around the early 1950s. There were many more greenhouses on Poplars Nursery than the one seen on the right of the painting. The Lombardy Poplars planted by Sheila's father can be seen at the top.

SHEILA, THE ENVIRONMENT LOVER

SHEILA WAS ALWAYS VERY AWARE OF AND tuned in to her environment. She was the eldest in her family and grew up at Poplars Nursery, the greenhouse business owned and built by her father Sidney. Sheila was born at home, where she lived all her early life, and where she was married. It was and still is a lovely place, with fields all around. It has now become a busy and successful garden centre, although the family no longer grow tomatoes and cucumbers for the commercial market.

After finishing school, and after a year as a secretary in Luton, and living at home, Sheila went to Homerton College in Cambridge — now part of Cambridge University, then a two-year teachers' training college. When she returned home in the summer after her first year at college, she found a change at the nursery. A small shed had appeared, and it was locked, and attached to the door was a notice stating — 'NO ADMITTANCE; DANGEROUS CHEMICALS.'

She asked her father what this meant. He said that the Department of Agriculture had been advising the greenhouse industry and farmers that chemicals were the "new way" to grow crops more easily and cheaply than the old ways; there would be no more pests, and the harvests would be better.

"But Dad," she said, "you never had trouble with pests. You used Bessie [their old steam tractor] to steam sterilize the greenhouse soil every winter, and to heat the greenhouses in spring, and you never had any disease. Why change now?"

I think Sidney answered something like, "It's the modern way. The department officials visited and explained it all. The experts know best." Sheila told me that she was quite upset, and argued her point, but the brave new world of post-war England was inexorably changing the rural life in England.

This was one of Sheila's favourite prayers or poems. I do not know where she originally found it.

A MANCHU SHAMAN'S PRAYER

Oh Lord of Heaven, Oh Manchu Leaders, Manchu Princes.
We pray to you for our swift horses.
Through your power, may their legs lift high, their manes toss.
May they swallow the winds as they race; and grow ever sleeker as they drink in the mists.
May they have fodder to eat; and be healthy and strong.
May they have roots to nibble and reach a great age.
Guard them from ditches and from precipices over which they might fall.
Keep them from thieves.
Oh Gods guard them.
Oh Spirits help them.

Sheila painted this the day after she had a particularly vivid dream involving horses and other animals and people. Horses were special for Sheila.

This was found on a torn piece of artist's paper. Sheila had been teaching at a school workshop. Somebody "saved" some of the scraps on the floor. This was one of the scraps.

A CERTAIN DISCIPLINE

This jewel-like home from Space depicted
We've treated as a garbage bin.
So live more lightly on the planet.
Embrace a certain discipline.

What each one does affects another
And not to care is truly sin.
So live more lightly on the planet.
Embrace a certain discipline.

An ocean burgeoning with plastic
Brings daily death to fish and fin
So live more lightly on the planet
Embrace a certain discipline.

Technology rapes field and forest;
Takes wealth, but does not put it in.
So live more lightly on the planet
Embrace a certain discipline.

Sustain community and living.
Aim to share, and not to win.
Live more lightly on the planet.
Embrace a certain discipline.

Poem found on the back of an envelope!

THE SKIER

There once was a skier so merry and bright
He paid all his money and learned to ski right.
The day was a wonder. The hills were sheer bliss;
But a pop can was waiting to change all of this.

He came down those hills just rejoicing to be
Alive and out skiing; So happy was he.
Then the tips of his skis in a pop can entangled
He fell with a thud, and his elbow was mangled.

Now how did that pop can come to be there?
Why! — a skier had thrown it while riding the chair.
Misery and grief can be caused by pop cans.
It should be recycled not thrown by his hands.

Poem found in a file among documents dating from 1989 to 1991:

TO AMY CROSS

Amy Willard Cross
My blessings go to you.
I'm really glad I'm here at home
Suffering from the "flu."
For had I gone outside
On my Environmental stroll
Why! I'd have missed your letter,
And another kindred soul.

I walk environmentally,
That's when I fill my sacks
With cans, and sets of plastic rings
From thrown away six packs.
With lube cans that the snowplough man
Has thrown into the ditch,
And sundry other items
That can make recyclers rich.

I feel so good and caring
Until I reach my door,
And edge my sacks into the porch.
There's no room anymore.
It's full of "other people's junk"
That's waiting for the day
I take it for recycling,
When my flu has gone away.

In bygone days I cleaned my rooms
And emptied garbage bins,
While listening to Morningside
Or planning various things.
But now I have to concentrate

And sort the messy stuff.
Is it P.E.T. or plastic?
Is the paper inked or rough?
Could this card be virgin fibre
Prized in the USA?
If I light my woodstove with it
I'll feel guilty all the day!

I know that many out there
Clean with vinegar and soda;
And compost all their kitchen scraps,
And love the compost odour.
But I have a lonesome feeling
At the checkout, when I see
That the only one with recycling bags
Invariably is me.

But I'll eat less meat; buy needs not wants
And stop my wasteful ways.
Leave home my car, except of course
On really awful days.
I heard David Suzuki say
We have to stop this madness,
It's a matter of survival.
So… I'll do it all with gladness.

A patient, and friend, stopped me one morning as I was going into the clinic and said,

"Is Sheila becoming a 'Bag Lady?' Are you encouraging her?"

"What are you talking about?" I said.

"Well, I saw her walking along the Trans-Canada Highway near Humber Village, and she was in the ditch picking up cans and bottles and trash."

"No. She's recycling!!" I said, "and just trying to clean up some of the mess."

MOBY JOE — Written 28 Feb 1967

In a pool near Burgeo
There's a whale called Moby Joe,
Cruising sadly to and fro,
Prisoner at Burgeo.

He did but a-hunting go
After shoals of herring oh;
Crossed a submerged ledge, and so
He's trapped in a pool in Burgeo.

Farley Mowat filled with woe,
Sent a wire to Premier Joe.
"Let Newfoundland her kindness show;
Please help our whale at Burgeo."

The Premier made provisions, so,
"Let all ye hardy fishers know
We'll pay ye well, go net and row
And drive fresh herring to Moby Joe."

Poor Moby Joe had felt so low,
Not a scrap had passed his Oesophago
Not a herring thrown by friend or foe
In his lonely pool at Burgeo.

Eighty tons of Moby Joe
With a cavernous Tum like a big round O.
Rumble, rumble, basso profundo
Echoing round the shores of Burgeo.

Twelve days are long and dreary oh.
And twelve nights dark and weary oh.
Far from home, and no place to go,
Waiting to die in Burgeo.

On the thirteenth day he lay below
The cold grey waters of Burgeo
Submerged and desolate, when rippling slow
The waters were cleaved by a dory oh.

And herrings, herrings, herrings, sparkling so
Swiftly came swimming into Burgeo.
Happy gourmet breakfast for Moby Joe
Donated by the boys in the dory oh.

Moby Joe, Moby Joe; hear him snort, hear him blow,
As he galumphs around the pond, wildly wildly to and fro.
Scares the hell out of the boys in the dory oh.
Newfoundland is glad to serve you. Mange Bien, Moby Joe.

Sadly, the tale ends on a grimmer note. Some men in Burgeo started using
Moby Joe as a target, and eventually the whale died.

THE EARTH IS OURS

This was written for an environmental conference that Sheila was asked to address in Grand Falls, either in 1991 or 1992. It was called "Caring for Creation," and it was organized by the Integrated Education Council. Sheila was invited as a guest speaker.

THE EARTH IS A HOME FOR ALL PEOPLE

When Eileen Colbourne phoned and asked me to speak on the Earth, as part of the theme "The Earth is a Home for all People," I was happy to say yes. For in every way, my relationship to the Earth and the life of the Earth is one that sustains me and brings my greatest joy and greatest feelings of belonging.

Eileen said, "I'm calling you now [this was early summer] to give you plenty of time" — Well, that was a blessing, but also a burden, for all this summer I have had this niggle at the back of my mind — "I have to get round to preparing this talk." So, as family commitments and visitors, and a very pressured part-time job filled the hot days, I became very tired, my back played up, and I was stressed out. The talk I had to prepare began to bring thoughts of panic. When will I ever have time to sit down quietly?

Anyhow, the time came when the visitors had gone, and I went to bed thinking, "Tomorrow I will have a day to myself — I will get down to it."

But when I awoke, I still felt tired; all I wanted was to sleep the day away.

Then — I began to hear rustlings and cheeping in the tall birch tree that grows right outside my window. It is a beautiful tree; the bark is very smooth and white, clean and strong, reaching to the blue sky. I had to get up and investigate. The tree was full of little birds, very young chickadees, and little brown and yellow birds.

They were prying under the white bark with their tiny beaks. Searching for insects, they flitted from twig to twig on their new little wings. One little chickadee whose feathers were all tiny and ruffled perched on the bottom window frame and pecked under the flaking wood, just inches from my hand, and there he found his breakfast.

I stood and watched them until the whole flock moved off to another tree.

This was such a wonderful moment; I don't know how long it lasted, but my tiredness vanished. The tiny birds brought such a sense of joy that I became a different person, feeling centred, at peace, and ready to begin writing of the Earth.

This moment speaks perfectly of what it means to find again the connectedness we have lost, and how when we open ourselves to be a part of all the life of the Earth, we are rewarded a thousand-fold. I think it illustrates the great power of healing and renewal that is waiting to restore us. My first impulse was to be very grateful for this gift.

We all know these moments when we feel at one with everything around us — perhaps by the ocean, soothed by the repetition of the waves washing in over the pebbles and seashells; perhaps in the quiet woods where the fragrant scents of the trees and earth are all around, and light dances between green leaves of birch and maple; and there is cool shade amongst the conifers; perhaps picking berries amongst the rocks and bushes, with big skies above, and a cool breeze blowing to keep the flies away.

These are moments of peace and true living. John Stewart Collis, in a book called *A Vision of Glory*, describes our connection to all of the Earth, and how we are of the same elements as the rocks around us. We breathe the oxygenated air created by green plants; we drink the waters cleansed by the Earth and pumped from deep down by the roots of trees, taken up through the branches to the leaves, lost from the leaves by transpiration, and dispersed as mist and clouds to fall again as rain. Since I read this, I have noticed the mist hanging above the trees at the tops of the mountains.

It is a circle.

The rain fills the rivers, nourishes the green plants, gives us water for our thirst, and waters the parched places so that all living things, plants, and animals may feed and grow.

We may buy our food in the store and forget all these connections, but if this circle of taking up and giving back of the waters were to cease, or be so polluted that falling rain would kill — where then would the fruit, the grains, the vegetables, the meat, and the fish be found? If the Earth and the sea are polluted, poisoned by our carelessness, then the cycle of life cannot sustain us. When we clear the forests we interfere, and the land becomes dry and blown away. The rain does not fall. Very little can live.

I have been searching through a book I own called *Earth Prayers from Around the World,* and there is one prayer written by a German woman who lived in the twelfth century: Hildegard of Bingen. She was a Christian mystic, head of a convent, and a very gifted woman. You may have heard some of the music she composed on a CBC *Ideas* program. There were very few outlets for brilliant women in the twelfth century, but in the convent her music was sung by the nuns in the chapel and thus preserved.

This is what she writes:

> The earth is at the same time mother.
> She is mother of all that is natural; mother of all that is
> human.
> She is mother of all,
> For contained in her are the seeds of all.
> The earth of humankind contains all moistness,
> All verdancy; all germinating power.
> It is in so many ways fruitful.
> All creation comes from it, yet it forms not only the basic
> raw material of
> Humankind.

We live in stressful times, and for an island people who for centuries have lived so close to the rhythms of the natural world, the cruel facts of the loss of the fishery, the breakup of family and community, and the loss of livelihood are so overwhelming that they seem at times insurmountable. We are not blameless, and we know that with many other nations we have overfished, and contaminated and polluted the waters with our garbage. Here is a prayer from the native Ojibway people:

> Grandfather look at our broken-ness
> We know that in all creation only the human family
> Has strayed from the Sacred Way.
> We know that we are the ones that are divided
> And we are the ones who must come back together

To walk the Sacred Way.
Grandfather, Sacred One, teach us to love compassion and honour
That we may heal the earth and heal each other.

We live in a portion of the Earth that many envy, and in our heart of hearts we know that we are richly blessed. Who would wish to be in any of the war-torn countries in our world, in the Middle East where religious fundamentalists are destroying people's lives, in Burma, in Tibet and Eastern China where the Chinese are cruelly destroying everything Tibetan, and Uigur. We know we are fortunate, but we forget. Sometimes we need space, and time alone, and Rabbi Nachman of Bratazlaw was well aware of that — not just alone, but in contact with the Earth.

Grant me the ability to be alone
May it be my custom to go outdoors every day
Amongst the trees and grasses,
Amongst all growing things, and there may I be alone,
And enter into prayer
To talk to the one I belong to.

Another young woman, also a Christian mystic, lived also in a time of trouble. Julian of Norwich lived in England during the fourteenth century, when England and France were fighting a war that dragged on for one hundred years. The Black Death stalked the land. The pestilence destroyed whole communities. The next village to where I grew up in England has an old church, and nothing else. Everybody died in the Black Death.

At this time there was very little food; it is described as a time of decline and corruption. When Julian was thirty years old, she had sixteen visions. She recorded them in her *Book of Showings*. She urged her fellow believers to look beyond their misfortunes, to look with compassion on their neighbours and to all in need.

She writes,

All goodness is God and
There is food, tasty and pleasing to the Lord.

Be a good gardener; dig and ditch, toil and sweat,
And turn the earth upside down.

So now I want to tell you about an American lady of this century
who would certainly have agreed with Saint Julian, as she became known,
although she found an improvement on the methods that Julian of Norwich
recommends.

Ruth Stout was a gardener, and when she moved to the country — to
Poverty Hollow, she was determined to grow everything she loved, not just
for her family, but for countless visitors as well. She set out and planted
huge gardens, toiled from morn to night, had some success, and all kinds
of failures, but mostly frustration and exhaustion. Because her garden was
large, she had to wait for somebody to plough it for her each spring, and
always the men were busy on the farm, and she had to wait.

Here she tells of a day of discovery for her:

> Now and then there is a morning so beautiful it
> makes you feel that all the world, and heaven too has had
> a conference and voted to create one perfect thing. When
> you have rejoiced in the splendour all round you, you close
> your eyes the better to drink in the sounds. There are not
> only birds singing and calling from the trees — there is
> also music in the grass. You are afraid to take a step for
> fear of treading upon some lovely and mysterious sound.
>
> On one of these brilliant mornings I wandered
> aimlessly over to the asparagus bed and said "Bless your
> heart, you don't have to wait for anyone to plough you."
>
> A thought struck me. "Why plough, Why plough? I
> am not going to. I am going to plant."
>
> It was my good fortune that I had formed the habit of
> leaving all the vegetable waste, such as corn stalks, right
> there in the garden, and had spread leaves all over it in the
> Fall, and vegetable garbage all winter long. Now when I
> raked this mass of stuff aside to make a row for the spinach
> I found the ground so soft that I made a tiny drill with my

finger. I didn't have a qualm, I felt so excited. It was like Columbus discovering America.

So she went ahead and planted.

Over the years she continued with her discovery. Anything she would have put on her compost heap — vegetable peelings, kitchen scraps (no animal matter) — went straight on her garden. She covered it all with straw, hay, leaves. Seaweed — as long as the mulch was six to eight inches deep.

She had wonderful results of huge healthy vegetables with a remarkable flavour, and No More Digging Ever!

She had discovered a way of gardening by mulching intensively. This enabled her to garden all her life. Here is her prescription for a long and happy life:

> I believe that growing old, from seventy to ninety, can be the most delightful part of a person's life. I believe there are two ways to grow old. One is to accept it and become more and more incapacitated, or to resent it and fight it all the way. Neither of these ways is for me, so I made out a plan of living, the keynote of which is enjoyment. I slowed up voluntarily.

And she did. She kept house, wrote gardening books, and grew vegetables and flowers, with the benefit of mulching. She froze all her winter vegetables; she made pickles and jams. When she felt tired, she took a nap.

People came from far and wide to learn from her. By nurturing the Earth, she lived lightly upon the Earth. She used no chemicals or pesticides. As she harvested, she returned all the residues. The earthworms and time did the rest.

Her garden was supremely healthy and vigorous, and so was she. She lived and gardened well into her nineties.

Ruth Stout's gardening methods emulate the way the forests maintain themselves.

The falling leaves and needles break down and form the forest loam, from which new life grows. When a fire sweeps through a forest, new nutrients such as potash become part of the mix, and blueberries and raspberries take over, until they are crowded out by new trees, and a new forest appears.

So, in our gardens we can mulch with seaweed and leaves and wood ash from the stove, and peelings from the kitchen — and perhaps live to ninety doing it.

So how can we live more lightly upon the Earth?

We can take responsibility.

It is heartening to see more boxes springing up for recycling, but how many people are using them?

In St Andrews in the Codroy Valley here in Newfoundland, there are boxes for cans, plastic, and paper; but when I go down to the beach, the charred remains of a beach bonfire are surrounded by aluminum cans and broken beer bottles. I take a bag and pick them up, but there will be more the next time I go. The last time I was down there, two young men from New York drove up. They did not comment, nor did they stay very long. They were neat and clean and had enjoyed Gros Morne, and they were on their way back to the ferry. I do not think they appreciated the broken bottles.

How do we get it into people's heads to take their litter home with them?

Anyhow, if you have an empty bag in your pocket always, it could make a difference if everybody set about cleaning up this beautiful part of the Earth we live in.

Also, walking and picking up litter is very good exercise for the waistline as well as the legs.

Cotton Bags. To pick up the groceries. These are mine. I have used them for more than five years [this was written around 1990]. They are very strong and hold more than plastic bags. If you work out how many bags it takes to bring home a week's groceries — say ten to make it easy — multiply by fifty-two weeks in a year = 520. Multiply by five (the years I have used cotton bags) = 2600. That means I have NOT brought home quite a lot of plastic bags.

When you go home, check how many plastic bags it takes for your family's groceries over a week. It's probably more than ten. I know there are boxes to recycle plastic bags, but have you actually seen a person putting bags in? I haven't. People must do so, but I haven't seen anyone. But where are the bags that are not recycled?

In the dump? Flapping in the bushes all the way to the dump?

Let us live more lightly on the Earth.

CODROY

Scenes from the Codroy Valley, where as a family
we spent our summer holidays.

In the Little Codroy Estuary: a fisherman's boathouse.

Irises in Northwest Cove: this small rivulet had so
many of these irises growing in and around it.

The Little Codroy Estuary.

Northwest Cove.

Looking from our cottage out to The Long Range Mountains.

MRS. CURTIS

SHEILA USED TO REGULARLY VISIT MRS. CURTIS, who then lived with her daughter Lily in Steady Brook. Occasionally Sheila took her daughters, and then there would be music. On one occasion Mrs. Curtis, with Sheila's help, drew a map of Pinchard's Island in Bonavista Bay with all the houses and the names of the residents. I remember Hounsells and Norrises as being prominent family names.

Mrs. Curtis had grown up there, as a child, and she remembered where they all had lived. The Anglican Church, which had been floated to Newtown after Pinchard's Island was resettled, is still in use.

Sheila wrote the following notes after a later visit to Mrs. Emily Curtis, who was now living in a long-term care home in Stephenville Crossing:

> Tears crumpled her old face when she saw me in the doorway. She sat bolt upright in her hard chair, back against the wall — as far from her ninety-nine-year-old roommate as possible — and so angled that the broad expanse of ocean reflecting up light under huge skies was excluded from her view.
>
> "I don't want to be here. I don't want to be here." I held her, sobbing. "Lily is going to try to get me out."
>
> In her chair opposite, the ancient French Canadian sat calmly by the window. The ledge was filled with small flower arrangements, photographs of grandchildren,

family weddings — and above the bed behind her a crucifix.

"Who is your friend, Mrs. Curtis?"

"Agatha Hawkins. She's deaf, poor old thing! She's ninety-nine."

Mrs. Hawkins told me of all her family, including their last visit and what she was knitting for the youngest. Yesterday twenty of them had visited her – together.

"Mrs. Curtis was so sick I thought she might die," said Mrs. Hawkins.

"Oh, my dear, you don't know. I thought I would die. My neck, my back – all down here," said Mrs. Curtis. The tears came again. "They all kissed me, twenty of them."

"Pull your chair forward and let me massage your neck. Where are the photographs of your family?"

"I forgot to bring them. I don't want to stay."

PORTRAITS

Sheila. Self-portrait. From the 1970s. It must be difficult
looking into a mirror to do self-portraits.

Sheila. Another self- portrait. This was a pen (or crayon)
and charcoal sketch. It is one of my favourites.

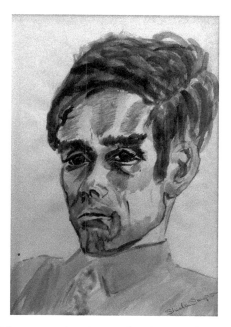

Ian. One of the many sketches and paintings that were made of
her family. This is Ian Simpson, her left-behind husband.

Angus, oldest son.

Mark. Possibly in a not-too-happy mood at having to sit still.

Rebecca, hair conscious age.

Robin and Rebecca. This picture was exhibited in St John's.

Sidney Little. Sheila's father, painted during a visit to Corner Brook.

Florence Little, Sheila's mother. Sadly, she died too young a short time after this visit. I think it is a remarkable likeness, but Florence did not like it and said she looked miserable. But she had a sad look for over a decade, since Sheila's younger sister Barbara had died. It is sad she did not like it.

Gerry Squires, one of Newfoundland's most famous and admired
painters. Gerry taught Sheila how to paint in water colours, and
under his inspiration her painting thrived. He lived and taught
in Corner Brook for a very short time in the early 1970s.

And this is Gail Squires, Gerry's wife. I think this is one of
Sheila's best paintings.
Thank you, Gerry and Gail.

A model at one of Gerry Squire's art classes. I cannot find out her name.

STILL LIFE

Lupins in our garden. I think Sheila seeded many
of the lupins all around Humber Village.

A view from 36 Raymond Heights looking down the Humber Arm to the
Blomidon Mountains.
This was our home till we moved to Humber Village, and into the forest!

Also a view from Raymond Heights. Although misty,
and perhaps mystical, I love this painting.

This was one of Sheila's first paintings in Newfoundland. It is "The
Prairie" in Stephenville Crossing. It looks over the Newfoundland
Railway which was still very active at that date, and out to the
Long Range Mountains. This was painted in 1963 or 1964.

(Still Life Photo 9)

A winter scene in Corner Brook, perhaps on the golf course.

FURTHER THOUGHTS

THERE IS A POEM WRITTEN AFTER SHEILA'S parents Florence and Sydney had dined in a "castle" in New England. But there is a story to tell first.

After Sheila's father Sydney retired (well, half-retired) from running Poplars, his nursery/garden centre, he swapped homes with John, his son, and moved into Toddington. John moved to Poplars.

Sydney became involved in horticultural projects in Toddington and did some landscaping restoration around Chalgrave church. Chalgrave church was built in the twelfth century and is just over a mile outside Toddington, and apart from a farm cottage, it is alone and isolated. The story is that after the Black Death in the Middle Ages, the few surviving villagers removed themselves from the doomed village and relocated in Tebworth, just a few miles away.

But Chalgrave remained a parish church. Although the land around had been owned by the Loring family for several generations, it was originally a feudal "gift" from the king, all starting from William the Conqueror.

One morning, Sydney had surprise visitors, who, with a strong American accent, asked if he was Sydney Little. These visitors were a Mister Lou Loring with his wife, from Massachusetts, USA. He had been to see the Chalgrave church, but he could not get in. The sexton cleaning up the graveyard suggested that he find Sydney, who had a key to the church as he was doing some work on the tower with the masons.

Mr. Loring explained that he had decided to try to trace his ancestors. His family had always known that the USA Lorings had arrived on the *Mayflower*. So, he had started his enquiries at Boston Spa in Lincolnshire, which was the port from which the *Mayflower* sailed. There is a museum there, and, sure enough, there was a Loring on the list.

I do not know how he linked his Lorings to Chalgrave in Bedfordshire. I suspect that the novels by Sir Arthur Conan-Doyle — *Sir Nigel Loring* and *The White Company*, a great historical read — might have been a source.

Sydney took the Lorings to the church and showed them around.

Chalgrave Church is a small gem. There are centuries-old wall paintings, and there are two large medieval tombs with Sir Nigel Loring in one and his wife in the other. Their outlines in carved relief are especially well preserved. The carvings indicate that she had a large family, in spite of Sir Nigel spending so much time out of the country on errands for the Black Prince (later King Edward).

He has a small dog carved under his feet. I was told that means that Sir Nigel was on the Crusades.

I imagine that the Lorings spent quite a lot of time at Chalgrave. Sydney and Florence invited them back for supper, and then they stayed the night.

Sydney and Florence's house — Toftrees — goes back hundreds of years. Most of the structure is Elizabethan or thereabouts. It has very low ceilings, narrow doors, and steep narrow stairs. It must have been a surprise for the Lorings.

When they left the next day, they told Sydney and Florence, "As you are going to visit your daughter and family in Newfoundland next year, why don't you spend another few days and come and visit us at Scituate, in Massachusetts?"

That is what occurred the next year. Sydney and Florence enjoyed this extension to their holiday. They were a little taken aback when the opulent building they were taken to turned out to be for visitors; the large main house was a little apart. They were also taken to Florida, where the Lorings have a winter home, and they visited the Space Center and watched a space launch. Sydney especially was very impressed and comfortable in the USA.

This is Sheila's second-hand impression:

> Oh, to dine at Scituate
> Off swordfish,
> On expensive plate.

Exquisite fish,
So delicate.
Not once, but twice
At Scituate.
But, – in a State where prices rise
At such a rate,
I'd surely hate
To foot the bill

And so, I'd take my reel and rod
And catch a little dish of scrod.
A tasty fish with name so odd,
And such a change from all this cod
That Newfoundland was given by God.

36 Raymond Heights
Corner Brook, Newfoundland
24th July 1969

Dear Mummy and Daddy,

In this, the first year of the "moon men," I pick up my pen to write to Sydney, who espoused Florence, and in the year before moon men, one thousand, nine hundred, and thirty-three, begat Sheila, who espoused Ian, and begat Angus; and they, finding the land wherein they were filled by many tribes, left their native land and journeyed to a Newfoundland. Standing there upon they found the land fair to look upon: the air clear and unpolluted, the trout streams sweet and fresh, and the pools wherein lurk the salmon in the quiet rivers, deep and cool, and beckoning to the heart of man.

Stay by my green stillness, breathe my clean air, travel my untrod ways, and make ye here a home for thy children.

And it was good, and of children there increased threefold: John Mark; Rebecca Mary; and Robin Fionna McDougalll Simpson were born in the new land.

And they laughed in the brisk cold snows of winter, and cast a lazy fly for fish that were unwary, and it was good.

But they missed in their hearts the smiles of their forefathers, they missed the loving speech, and the children sighed: "When will they come? When will they come?"

And once they came for three good weeks, and the children laughed, and the boys fished with their grandfather, and the little girl cuddled up to her grandmother, sitting on a knee which had comforted other little girls, now grown.

But the three weeks passed so quickly, like the life of a butterfly bright in the summer months; and the Great bird took them high in the sky, and they were gone.

Grandpa, we will keep your rod for next time, next time. Grandma, your sunhat, faded from the Newfoundland sun, waits for you at the cottage. Grandma, we have another little girl for you to cuddle. Come again. Come again.

Sheila

Letter written by Sheila to induce a second visit to Newfoundland. And it worked. They came.

TO MY FATHER ON HIS 83ᴿᴰ BIRTHDAY

If I could remember figures
I'd be certain of your age.
I know it's over 80,
Which makes you wise and sage.

But the Sage of Lewis Carroll
Used to stand upon his head.
My distant sources tell me
You do needlepoint instead.

He kept his limbs quite supple,
With ointment from a jar.
You exercise your ankle
When driving in your car.

But I've not heard them mention
If that sage, as locks grew greyer
Could build hexagonal tables,
Or design and build a stair.

If they could, they failed to tell me
How he piloted a plane,
And ascended by balloon
To study the terrain.

I don't think he took his grandson
Mounting spirals in a glider,
Or flew a Tiger Moth, plus daughter,
With a camera beside her.*

Of course that was a time ago,
But it's my claim to fame
When we made our contribution
In the Archaeology game.

The years have brought their joys,
And the years have brought their tears
When dear wife and daughter died,
And you, lonely, faced the years.

But with Mary at your side,
You have love again and smiles.
And music lifts the rafters,
And reverberates the tiles.

So, I wish you birthday happiness
With family and friends,
And as all good things have to,
This is where my poem ends.

* To photograph the Beaker sites while leaning over in the streaming air
and hanging on the rigging.

TO TOM

Oh Tom! I often wonder how you've survived so long
In a union with my sister – who's so forceful and so strong.
But you've made it up to fifty-five,
Still thriving and alive,
Despite the way she treats you when Canadians arrive.
For she left a message for us that disturbs me to this day -
It's here for your perusal. Construe it as you may!

There's soup in the saucepan
Cheese (sic) in the fridge
Tom's in the bottom of fridge
Help yourself.

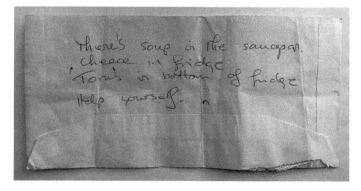

"Toms" were how the Little family referred to
tomatoes. "Cucs" were cucumbers.

SHEILA'S VALENTINE'S DAY POEM

THIS IS THE POEM THAT WON THE Corner Brook Physicians Valentine's Day party prize — a bottle of wine. I think it took place in the mid-1980s.

If you were the last cod in the ocean,
I just could not care for you more;
So, I'm thinking about conservation
Of the Valentine that I adore.

Some say it's because of the foreigners
That there are no more fish in the sea,
So, I'll establish some boundaries
To your accessibility.

Let me think – I must limit attention
From Senoras Portuguese or from Spain,
And from any Mamselles of the French kind
Who might want to addle your brain.

Since they gave you your badge for Alzheimer's
And you wear it most of the time,
I'll constantly have to remind you
You're an Oldie and Goldie BUT MINE!

Now I know there's concern for the species;
The marine kind I hasten to add,
But there's no fun in this Ms. Conception *
You're a great Biological Dad.

Though I think you should speak to your daughters
And have a quick word with the boys,
And tell them you're ready and willing
To partake of Grandfatherly joys.

I think that a little more swimming
Would keep that old body in trim,
Though you tell me that you get your exercise
When playing on your violin.

And your lungs benefit from singing,
So it's good that you sing in the choir
Though it makes you so late on a Monday
As I sit with a book by the fire.

Some say it's the cold in the water
That is decimating the fish;
So I prescribe half a bottle of red wine
To be taken whenever you wish.

It will warm you from inner to outside,
And ward off all agues and chills.
And make sure again in the summer
That we'll walk with the dogs on the hills.

Now the reason this Valentine's so enormous
Is to show how much I love you,
And in case you've forgotten your glasses
Which, my dear, you so frequently do,

For you just couldn't be more worth saving,
Or more important to me
If you were the last cod in the ocean,
Or the very last fish in the sea.

* TV show Jan 24th

Poem by a very excited Grandma Sheila, age seventy, waiting for her party to begin:

> Everybody says it's my party.
> But everybody says "Go away"
> I'm sitting here so very excited,
> While everybody else goes to play.
>
> I've brushed my hair and put my party dress on.
> I've smiled at everybody, but they say
> "Be good now, remember it's your party;
> Go away, go away, go away."
>
> They only let me stay with the children,
> As long as they're asleep and cannot talk.
> They tell me "Just be a real Good Grandma,
> And wear some clothes in which you can walk."
>
> I mustn't say, or use the wheelbarrow
> It's a No No.
> I mustn't leave the house till they say
> It had better be a really good party.
> "Be good now. Go away, Go away, Go away."

Found among a lot of Sheila's papers, probably written about 2004 or 2005.

> Little Tess Amelia
> Driving in her car
> Driving in the Kitchen,
> Far, far, far.
>
> First she takes a Groovy girl,
> Then she takes another.
> Down to see her Grandma,
> Then back to her mother.

Tess Amelia now growing up, and learning to bake from Sheila.
Tess grew up close to Sheila. She is now my co-
editor; she looks after the computer.

COMPETITION

What secret lure have fishes got
That I have not?

My husband has a tropical tank
With water-weed a vivid green.
An aerator runs non-stop,
And fishes swim from bottom to top,
Some flat, some long and lean.
But do those fishes cook and clean?

Some fishes swim with flirting tails,
Like glowing silk or satin.
The males, radiant and many-hued;
The smaller females less imbued.
They wear their wavy pattern;
But do they feed the dog, or let the cat in?

The fish get pregnant all the time
And swim with bulging tummies.
The mothers can't be with their young
They eat their babies just for fun.
Do fish make loving mummies?

He feeds them bits of puppy food
And crumbles it quite small.
He watches as they take each bit.
For hours beside the tank he'll sit
Watching them, that's all.
What secret lure have fishes got,
That I have not?

When he came home at any hour
Before we had the fish,
He'd say "Hello" – give me a kiss.

It's little things like that I miss,
I almost wish I were a fish.
What secret lure have fishes got
That I have not?

This poem was probably written in the mid-1970s.

The following poem was written in the year after Al Pittman died. Sheila and I attended the funeral ceremony and the scattering of Al's ashes. March Hare Day was the poetry festival in Corner Brook that Al helped to found and organize. It went on for several years after Al died.

Al was a very good author and poet.

POEM FOR AL PITTMAN

The Poets were gathered honouring Al.
But on this March Hare Day
I walked by the Humber,
And paused where the river
Had borne Al's ashes away.
The sky was blue
And river too.
Brown grass
And winter's old snow.
No living thing,
Just me and my dog
And the water's gentle flow.

Then this was strange.
As I thought of Al,
Birds arrived from everywhere.
All the promise of Spring
In their flight and song
So many suddenly
There.

Just in this place
Where we gathered for Al
Ducks swam and
Circled and dived.
Riding the wind there were
Ravens and Gulls,

In the alders, small birds
With their kind.

They stayed for a while
Five minutes or ten
Then no more
They were gone.
And the Poets remembered Al with their words
While the River flowed on and on.

TRIBUTES AND CONDOLENCES

MARK'S TRIBUTE, given at Sheila's funeral

I wasn't sure how to put this tribute together until yesterday morning when I took a walk through the garden and home of Mum and Dad. Everything you encounter says something about Sheila (our mum).

At the bottom of the garden stands a beautiful tall pine tree. It dominates the view and forty years ago was one of the reasons why Mum and Dad placed our house where it stands today. Between the pine tree and the house are flowerbeds full of blues and yellows amid mature maple and birch trees. Rose bushes line the path nearby. Mum loved nature and the trees and wildflowers were intentionally left.

In the summer the area is full of floral smells which Mum enjoyed and often commented on. Nearby is the site of Mum's old vegetable garden with its old compost heaps. Sheila loved gardening and we were the beneficiaries of many delicious meals from her garden. She was an organic gardener — No pesticides — No fertilizers. This was for our health and for the good of the environment which Mum cared about deeply. She was a principled person. Her old clothesline strung between two birch trees stands nearby. (No electrical dryer for my mother.)

Entering Mum and Dad's front porch, you are instantly aware that dogs live here. Mum loved her dogs. To Mum, dogs were friends and members of the family. She walked them daily for most of her life. I spoke with her sister, Margaret, on the phone two days ago. She told me that one of her clearest memories of Sheila long ago is of her sitting in the grass hugging her dog Topaz.

Moving past the porch, you enter the living room and on a shelf are pictures of Mum's grandchildren: Katie, Ainslie, Tess, Heidi, Jenni, and Ian. She loved her grandchildren and I picture her sitting with them drawing, painting, doing crafts, singing, or laughing as the children played dress-up. Very often Mum would take one wide-eyed grandchild upstairs to look through treasures from her childhood and early days in England. Mum loved history and the treasures included very old coins, arrowheads, and stories to go with them. Mum's younger brother John recently said this about her:

> Sheila had a great interest in antiquities and I recall her helping with an Archeological dig locally and then doing her own excavations in a corner of our land where she was very excited to find a flint arrowhead and evidence of napping.

All around the walls and window sills of Mum and Dad's home are paintings, pottery, and beautiful ornaments. Many of the paintings and the pottery pieces were created by Mum's own hands. There are beautiful water colours of mountains, oceans, and trees from different places Mum had lived in or visited in Newfoundland. Years ago, Angus, Rebecca, Robin, Dad, or I were often the subjects of her portraits... I think sometimes it may have taken some coaxing or other incentives to get us to remain still.

An old Scrabble board and battered Oxford Dictionary poke out from under one of the couches in the living room. Mum and Dad loved words and would have many intense and highly competitive games of Scrabble in the evenings. Often, good-natured arguments would occur over the validity of a word. The dictionary was always nearby to settle the discussion. The book became very tattered and worn.

Not far away in the kitchen is a shelf full of recipe books. The best of these are in the same condition as the Oxford dictionary. Mum was a fantastic and well-read cook. She invented and improvised in the kitchen based on experience and reading. She made wonderful healthy meals for years. Often at the end of a great meal, however, her love of her dogs would prevent one of us from getting the final tasty mouthful as Mum would vigorously defend the dog's right to a treat. We were also spoiled with homemade bread. I remember when we lived on Raymond Heights in Corner Brook, our paper boys would longingly comment on the smell of baking bread when they collected their weekly payment from the Simpson house.

At the top of the stairs there are pictures of Angus, Rebecca, Robin, and me from our early school years. We all have our favourite memories of Mum, but I know we would all agree on two things:

- She seemed to have a sixth sense for knowing if one of us was unhappy or in trouble.

- She read aloud beautifully. John, Mum's brother, agreed and sent me the following recollection:

> When I was a child, Sheila was like a mother to me. As the oldest of four children, she was always expected to take responsibility for the rest of
> us, and being ten years older than me, by the time I was four she would have been fourteen and I remember fondly her soft voice reading me bedtime stories.

Angus, Rebecca, Robin, and I all remember that same soft voice…

I wish I had the time to speak of Mum's courage and adventurous spirit in leaving England with a young family to live in out-port Newfoundland or to speak of her passion and commitment to causes she believed in. But I must end now.

Sheila was a beautiful, loving, caring, and highly principled person. She has left her mark deeply on our home and in our hearts. We have many memories to cherish. We love you, Mum, and will miss you.

CONDOLENCES FROM A GOOD FRIEND

She was indeed a remarkable woman. I so much enjoyed my last visit with you and Sheila. We toured through your house and I got a chance to see many of Sheila's magnificent paintings that adorn your walls.

The paintings were so expressive and brought out the true Sheila, the vibrant character who could so vividly express herself. Speaking of expressing herself, she was no shrinking violet. Even in her early stages of Alzheimer's, she could hold an audience and get her point across.

I remember an occasion, Ian, when you and I were scheduled to be doing a forty-minute presentation at the Stephenville Town Hall to a gathering of mayors and councillors who were members of the Southwest Coast Council.

A very ill-mannered mayor was chairing the meeting and he tried to cut Sheila off while she was expressing her feelings about protecting our coastlines from the hazards of fracking. Sheila was having none of this rudeness and petulant behaviour. She continued on, despite the mayor's displeasure, and finished making her point.

I would have loved to have known Sheila in her prime. She was a brilliant, artistic lady and she will be missed. The Corner Brook scene has lost a lovely lady.

This prayer was sent to me after Sheila's funeral. As an avid gardener, Sheila would have appreciated it and loved it:

Let us give thanks for a bounty of people:

Let us give thanks

For children who are our second planting, and, though they grow like weeds and the wind too soon blows them away, may they forgive us our cultivation and fondly remember where their roots are.

For generous friends... with hearts as big as hubbards and smiles as bright as their blossoms;

For feisty friends as tart as apples;

For continuous friends, who, like scallions and cucumbers, keep reminding us we had them;

For crotchety friends, as sour as rhubarb and as indestructible;

For handsome friends, who are as gorgeous as eggplants and as elegant as a row of corn — and the others — as plain as potatoes, and so good for you.

For funny friends, who are as silly as brussels sprouts and as amusing as Jerusalem artichokes, and serious friends as complex as cauliflowers and as intricate as onions;

For friends as unpretentious as cabbages, as subtle as summer squash, as persistent as parsley, as delightful as dill, as endless as zucchini, and who — like parsnips — can be counted on to see you through the long winter;

For old friends, nodding like sunflowers in the evening-time, and young friends coming on as fast as radishes;

For loving friends, who wind around us like tendrils, and hold us despite our blights, wilts, and witherings;

And finally, **for those friends now gone**, like gardens past, that have been harvested — but who fed us in their times that we might have life thereafter;

For all these we give thanks.

LAST WORDS

TOWARD THE END OF HER LIFE, SHEILA became less communicative and more and more confused. And in the last few weeks she hardly responded verbally. We brought the bed downstairs just over two weeks before she died. This was because we would suddenly miss her, and find her halfway upstairs clinging to the railing. It was only then that she started to become incontinent.

It was a time that pulled the family closer together. Mark would drive the four-to-five-hour journey almost every week when his shifts as park warden allowed, and he would often bring one of his children. About a week before Sheila died, Mark and I were at her bedside when the phone rang. It was her younger sister Margaret. I saw Sheila looking at me and I asked her if she wanted to "listen to your sister Margaret."

"I wondered when you would ask," she said. This was the best conversation I had had for weeks!

I gave her the phone, and Mark and I listened to what appeared to be one half of a normal, rational conversation. The next day, I phoned Margaret. She said "It was as if Sheila's Alzheimer's had disappeared. It was the best talk we've had for a couple of years."

I did not get any more talk from Sheila till four nights before she died. I was with her. Realizing that she was sleeping quietly and did not need anything, I lay down alongside her and fell asleep. When I woke, she was looking at me with wide open eyes. She had a look that I had seen a few months previously. On that occasion she had said, "Who are you? Am I married to you?" I beat her to the conversation this time.

"It's me, Ian," I said. "I just lay down for companionship. I was tired."

There was a long pause. She just kept looking at me.

"I do love you," she said. There was a pause, and then, "You've been so very kind to me." I was beginning to tear up then. Another long pause.

"You've looked after me," and she turned over and went back to sleep.

These were the last words between Sheila and me, although in the two years since her death, and especially while compiling this book, it is as if I am still having an ongoing conversation with her in my head. And it is very pleasant and good for me.

CPSIA information can be obtained
at www.ICGtesting.com
Printed in the USA
BVHW020952120621
609226BV00002B/3